EARTH

by Mary Lindeen

NORWOODHOUSE PRESS

DEAR CAREGIVER, The *Beginning to Read—Read and Discover Science* books provide young readers the opportunity to learn about scientific concepts while simultaneously building early reading skills. Each title corresponds to three of the key domains within the Next Generation Science Standards (NGSS): physical sciences, life sciences, and earth and space sciences.

The NGSS include standards that are comprised of three dimensions: Crosscutting Concepts, Science and Engineering Practices, and Disciplinary Core Ideas. The texts within the *Read and Discover Science* series focus primarily upon the Disciplinary Core Ideas and Crosscutting Concepts—helping readers view their world through a scientific lens. They pique a young reader's curiosity and encourage them to inquire and explore. The Connecting Concepts section at the back of each book offers resources to continue that exploration. The reinforcement activities at the back of the book support Science and Engineering Practices—to understand how scientists investigate phenomena in that world.

These easy-to-read informational texts make the scientific concepts accessible to young readers and prompt them to consider the role of science in their world. On one hand, these titles can develop background knowledge for exploring new topics. Alternately, they can be used to investigate, explain, and expand the findings of one's own inquiry. As you read with your child, encourage her or him to "observe"—taking notice of the images and information to formulate both questions and responses about what, how, and why something is happening.

Above all, the most important part of the reading experience is to have fun and enjoy it!

Sincerely,

Shannon Cannon, PhD
Literacy Consultant

Norwood House Press
For more information about Norwood House Press please visit our website at www.norwoodhousepress.com or call 866-565-2900.
© 2022 Norwood House Press. Beginning-to-Read™ is a trademark of Norwood House Press. All rights reserved. No part of this book may be reproduced or utilized in any form or by any means without written permission from the publisher.

Editor: Judy Kentor Schmauss   **Designer:** Sara Radka

Photo Credits: Getty Images: cover, 1, 3, 4, 6, 7, 9, 10, 11, 12, 14, 18, 20, 22, 23, 26, 28, 29; Shutterstock: 6, 6, 7, 8, 9, 10, 11, 16, 22, 23, 25, 29

Library of Congress Cataloging-in-Publication Data
Names: Lindeen, Mary, author.
Title: Earth / by Mary Lindeen.
Description: Chicago : Norwood House Press, [2022] | Series: Beginning-to-read | Audience: Grades K-1 | Summary: "Earth is one of eight planets and the only one with one moon. Its seven continents are made up of many different types of landforms, and they are surrounded by the oceans. Includes science and reading activities and a word list"— Provided by publisher.
Identifiers: LCCN 2021019420 (print) | LCCN 2021019421 (ebook) | ISBN 9781684508280 (hardcover) | ISBN 9781684046546 (paperback) | ISBN 9781684046607 (epub)
Subjects: LCSH: Earth (Planet)—Juvenile literature.
Classification: LCC QB631.4 .L56 2022 (print) | LCC QB631.4 (ebook) | DDC 550—dc23
LC record available at https://lccn.loc.gov/2021019420
LC ebook record available at https://lccn.loc.gov/2021019421

Library ISBN: 978-1-68450-828-0   Paperback ISBN: 978-1-68404-654-6

This is planet Earth.

The blue parts are the ocean.

The greenish-brown parts are the land.

Earth has seven continents.

Each one is a giant piece of land.

North America

Europe

South America

Asia

Africa

Australia

Antarctica

desert

plateau

canyon

mountains

Earth's land has many different forms.

hills

butte

prairie

island

All kinds of animals
and plants live
on the land.

snail

rabbit

grasshopper

mouse

sea turtle

eels

All kinds of animals and plants live in the ocean, too.

lobster

octopus

Different parts of
the ocean have
different names.

Atlantic
Ocean

Pacific Ocean

Arctic Ocean

Indian Ocean

Southern Ocean

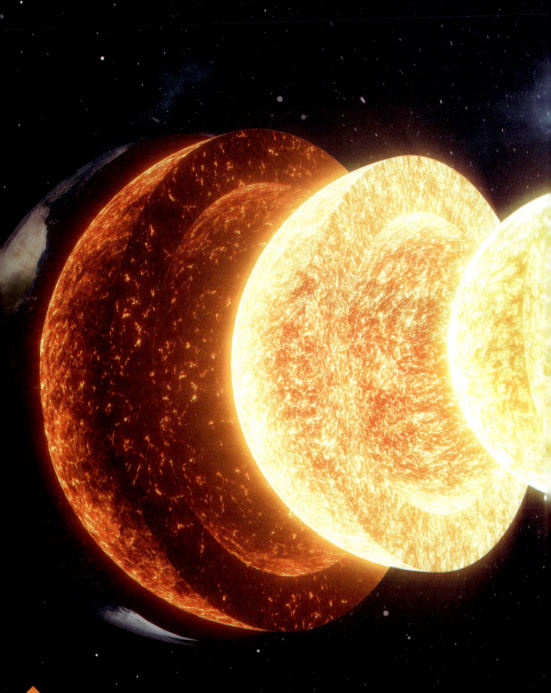

Under the land and
the ocean is a
layer of hot
melted rock.

Sometimes the melted rock comes up to the surface.

It comes out of a volcano as lava.

Cooled lava turns into hard rock.

This new rock makes new land.

Layers of gas surround Earth.

The layers are called the atmosphere.

The air we breathe is in the atmosphere.

sunny

rainy

foggy

snowy

Our weather also happens in the atmosphere.

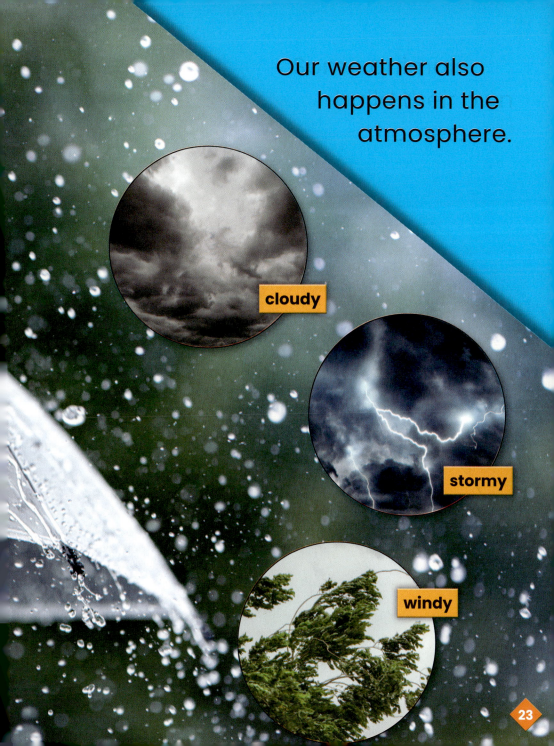

cloudy

stormy

windy

Earth has a sunrise every morning...

and a sunset every night.

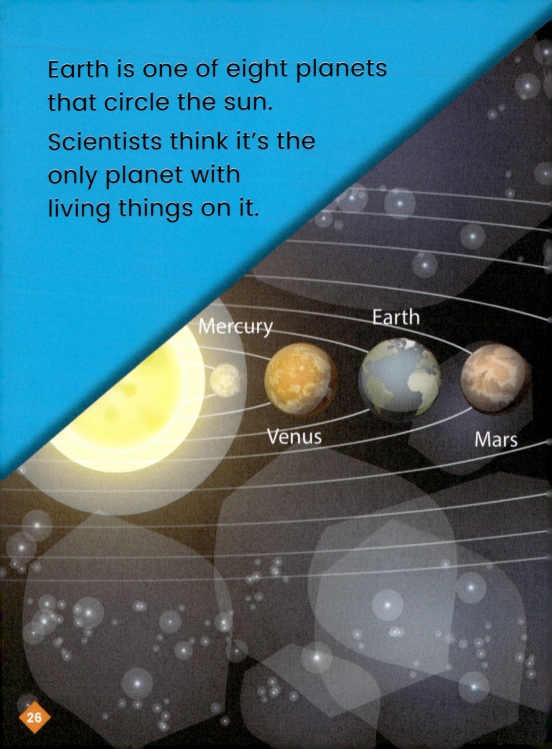

Earth is one of eight planets that circle the sun.

Scientists think it's the only planet with living things on it.

Mercury

Earth

Venus

Mars

Earth is also the only planet with just one moon.

You can get a great view of Earth from there!

Earth

...READING REINFORCEMENT...

CONNECTING CONCEPTS

CLOSE READING OF NONFICTION TEXT

Close reading helps children comprehend text. It includes reading a text, discussing it with others, and answering questions about it. Use these questions to discuss this book with your child.

- What are the greenish-brown parts of planet Earth?
- How many continents are there? How many can you name?
- What can be found under the land and ocean?
- What is lava?
- What is the atmosphere?

SCIENCE IN THE REAL WORLD

Use a world map or a globe to help your child find where you live. Then help them identify Earth's continents, oceans, and mountains and talk about the characteristics of where you live in relation to the information in the book.

SCIENCE AND ACADEMIC LANGUAGE

Make sure your child understands the meaning of the following words:

planet	continents	forms	volcano	lava
gas	atmosphere	sunrise	sunset	scientists

Have him or her use the words in a sentence.

FLUENCY

Help your child practice fluency by using one or more of the following activities:

1. Reread the book to your child at least two times while he or she uses a finger to track each word as it is read.

2. Read a line of the book, then reread it as your child reads along with you.

3. Ask your child to go back through the book and read the words he or she knows.

4. Have your child practice reading the book several times to improve accuracy, rate, and expression.

FOR FURTHER INFORMATION

Books:

Baumann, Anne-Sophie. *The Ultimate Book of Planet Earth*. San Francisco: Chronicle Books, 2019.

Blackall, Sophie. *If You Come to Earth*. San Francisco: Chronicle Books, 2020.

Sayre, April Pulley. *Thank You, Earth*. New York, NY: Greenwillow Books, 2018.

Websites:

National Geographic Kids: Facts About the Earth
https://www.natgeokids.com/au/discover/science/space/facts-about-the-earth/

NASA Science Space Place: All About Earth
https://spaceplace.nasa.gov/all-about-earth/en/

nineplanets.org: Earth Facts for Kids
https://nineplanets.org/kids/earth/

Earth uses the 101 words listed below. *High-frequency* words are those words that are used most often in the English language. They are sometimes referred to as sight words because children need to learn to recognize them automatically when they read. *Content* words are any words specific to a particular topic. Regular practice reading these words will enhance your child's ability to read with greater fluency and comprehension.

HIGH-FREQUENCY WORDS

a	can	have	new	the	up
air	come(s)	in	of	there	water
all	different	into	on	they	we
also	each	is	one	things	were
and	every	it	only	think	with
are	from	just	our	this	years
as	get	make(s)	out	to	you
blue	great	many	part(s)	too	
called	has	name(s)	that	under	

CONTENT WORDS

ago	eight	kinds	night	sunrise
animals	forms	land	ocean	sunset
atmosphere	gas	lava	piece	surface
breathe	giant	layer(s)	planet(s)	surround
circle	greenish-brown	live	plants	turns
connected	happens	living	rock	two-thirds
continents	hard	melted	scientists	view
cooled	hot	millions	seven	volcano
covers	huge	moon	sometimes	weather
Earth('s)	it's	morning	sun	

About the Author

Mary Lindeen is a writer, editor, parent, and former elementary school teacher. She has written more than 100 books for children and edited many more. She specializes in early literacy instruction and books for young readers, especially nonfiction.

About the Advisor

Dr. Shannon Cannon is an elementary school teacher in Sacramento, California. She has served as a teacher educator in the School of Education at UC Davis, where she also earned her PhD in Language, Literacy, and Culture. As a member of the clinical faculty, she supervised pre-service teachers and taught elementary methods courses in reading, effective teaching, and teacher action research.